D0577107

Published by Creative Education
123 South Broad Street, Mankato, Minnesota 56001
Creative Education is an imprint of The Creative Company

Designed by Stephanie Blumenthal
Production Design by Patricia Bickner Linder

Photographs by: FPG International, KAC Productions, and Tom Stack & Associates

Library of Congress Cataloging-in-Publication Data

Gish, Melissa and Nancy J. Shaw.
Fossils / by Melissa Gish and Nancy J. Shaw
p. cm. — (Let's Investigate)
Includes glossary.
Summary: Describes fossil discoveries, how and when they were made, and what
they tell us about Earth's history.
ISBN 0-88682-987-9
1. Fossils—Juvenile literature.   [1. Fossils.]
I. Title.   II. Series: Let's Investigate (Mankato, Minn.)
QE714.5.S473   1999
560—dc21   98-9329

First edition

2 4 6 8 9 7 5 3

FOSSILS

MELISSA GISH & NANCY J. SHAW

Creative Education

FOSSIL
FIND

One of the rarest fossil finds was made in 1922. Fossilized eggs and dinosaur skeletons were found together in a large deposit in Mongolia.

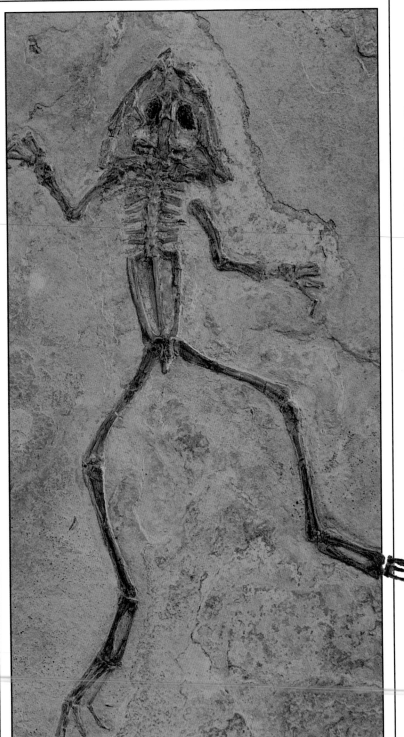

Above, starfish fossil; right, frog fossil

Like pages in a giant history book telling us about past life on Earth, fossils are the remains of living things preserved from an ancient time. They are the existing evidence on which our planet's **time chart**—the calendar of earth's history—was created.

Long ago, many plants and animals were buried without decaying and now remain as part of the earth's crust, creating what scientists call the **fossil record.**

There are three types of fossils. When only the hard parts of an animal—the teeth, bones, or shells—are preserved, the remains are called **body fossils.** Marks left by animal activity, such as footprints, are **trace fossils.** Molds of leaves and other very thin things are called **imprints.**

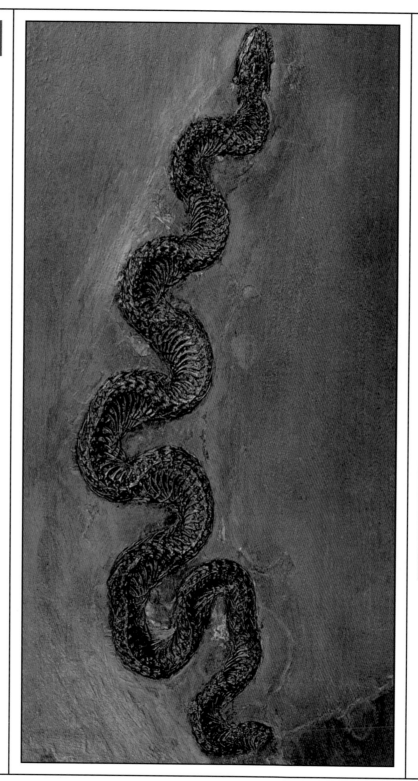

FOSSIL
SPEED

Scientists studying dinosaur footprints determined that the Tyrannosaurus rex could run up to 30 miles per hour (48 km/h).

5

Left, fossilized snake; above, an ammonite

FOSSIL COUSIN

*The nautilus is the closest modern descendent of the extinct **ammonites**, a group of marine mollusks with coiled shells containing many chambers.*

Scientists can tell many things about our planet from the fossil record. For example, fossils of tropical plants have been found in the Arctic, telling us that these places were once warm lands. Fossils also give us clues about the **evolution** of plants and animals. We now know that plants once lived only in the water. Ferns were the first plants to grow on dry land, just 400 million years ago. They evolved into the forests that cover our planet today.

Above, an ammonite turned to mineral; right, outside and inside of a fossilized pine cone

FOSSIL

E R A

*The **Paleozoic Era** is the first and longest era for which a large fossil record exists. It lasted from 600 million to 225 million years ago.*

Left, a horsetail plant

FOSSIL FORMS

When an animal such as a dinosaur died, it may have become buried in mud, lava, or sand. Over millions of years, layers of mud and sand built up. As the weight of these layers pressed down on the animal, **minerals** in the water soaked into the bones. Over time, this changed them into stone that became a **fossilized** skeleton.

FOSSIL

WING

The extinct Meganeura had a wingspan of 27 inches (69 cm). It was the largest winged insect ever known on earth.

Above, dragonfly fossil; top right, petrified wood; bottom right, stingray fossil

ossilized trees are also formed in this way. They became **petrified.** Huge petrified trees can be seen in Yellowstone National Park and in the Petrified Forest National Park in Arizona.

The La Brea Tar Pits in Los Angeles, California, were a burial ground for woolly mammoths, saber-toothed cats, and other animals that became trapped in the sticky pits. Thousands of fossilized bones have been pulled from these tar pits, and many still remain to be discovered.

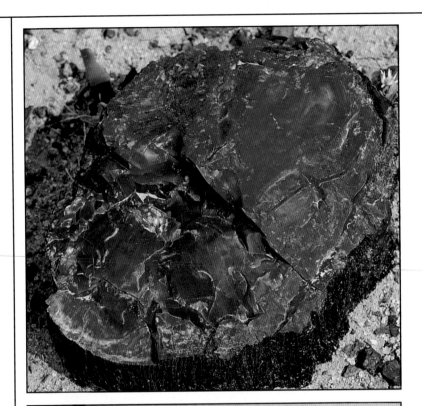

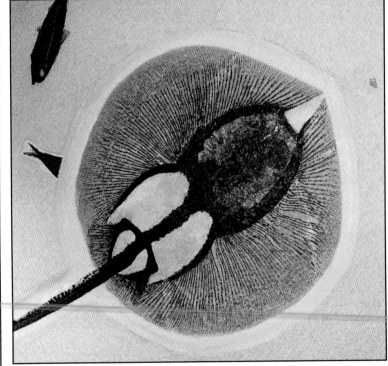

Some fossils are simply tracks pressed into mud. Long ago, the dinosaurs' footprints filled with sand that, over time, hardened into the rock we call sandstone. These fossils tell us the shape of a certain dinosaur's feet and sometimes even the animal's weight. Scientists who study only these types of fossils are called ichnologists.

There were 4,000 species of trilobites, insect-like creatures capable of curling their bodies up for protection.

Left, dinosaur track; above, trilobites

FOSSIL
FACT

A nest of unhatched dinosaur eggs was recently discovered in the Gobi Desert, apparently having been buried in an ancient sandstorm.

Fern leaf

The imprints of plants are often found preserved in coal or shale. Two hundred million years ago, when plants died and fell into the swamp, they slowly changed into peat, which then was covered with mud and sand. After millions of years, the weight of the mud layers finally turned the peat into coal. These imprints often look as if they were "painted" on the rocks.

The teeth and bones of prehistoric animals are so numerous in some areas that they form large deposits called "bone beds."

11

SPECIAL FOSSILS

Sometimes **ancient** insects became trapped in sticky tree sap which hardened into a clear, golden fossil called amber. Finding an insect inside amber is very rare and is considered a valuable discovery because it is really two fossils in one!

Left, winged termite trapped in amber; below, fossilized crinoids

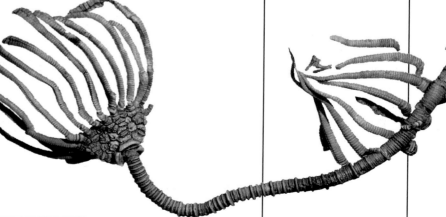

FOSSIL
FLYERS

*Many paleontologists believe that birds evolved from dinosaurs, making them the nearest relatives of ancient **reptiles.***

Fossil remains are sometimes found frozen instead of preserved in stone, tar, coal, or amber. Early species of bison, rhinoceros, and even prehistoric humans have been found. A woolly mammoth, an ancient cousin of the elephant, was discovered frozen in the Siberian ice in 1901. The mammoth's fur, tusks, organs, and blood were all preserved, and researchers who tasted the 25,000-year-old meat found that it was perfectly edible!

Above, bird fossil; top right, scientist assembling fossils in a lab; bottom right, scientist assembling a dinosaur

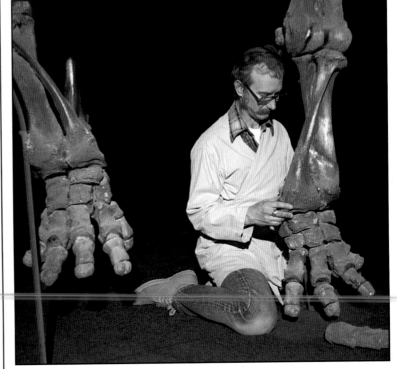

The study of the fossil record is called paleontology, and scientists in this field are paleontologists. They know where to find fossils and how to collect them without damaging them. Some of the most abundant fossil finds are discovered along coastal areas, sea cliffs, and rock quarries.

FOSSIL
LAKESIDE

Some of the world's oldest fossils are found on the north shore of Lake Superior. The well-preserved bacteria and blue-green algae fossils are about two billion years old.

13

Left, dinosaur quarry at Dinosaur National Monument, Utah; above, a fossilized shark tooth

The greatest amount of information on plant and animal relationships comes from studying tar seeps such as the La Brea Tar Pits in Los Angeles, California.

14

Paleontologists learn what ancient climates were like, and they now understand that species evolved when plants and animals tried new ways of living in changing environments. Scientists use **trilobite** fossils to determine the ages of different rocks on earth. With each new fossil discovery we learn important information about evolving **ecosystems.**

FOSSIL

F A C T

The first flying animals with a backbone were pterosaurs. Their name means "winged lizard," and their fossils date back to 200 million years ago.

Far left, a trilobite; left, plant imprints left on coal

Often when land is leveled by bulldozers for building railroads, highways, or buildings, fossils are found. Many new fossil discoveries are made all the time in canyons and stream beds, where **erosion** from wind and water peel away the layers of rock and earth.

16

The Grand Canyon, in Arizona, is a favorite fossil hunting site. A descent into the canyon is like a journey back through time, from 600 million to 200 million years ago. The farther down you go, the older the fossilized life forms are. At the very bottom there are no fossils at all—it is some of the oldest rock exposed anywhere on earth.

Right, Grand Canyon; far right, crinoids

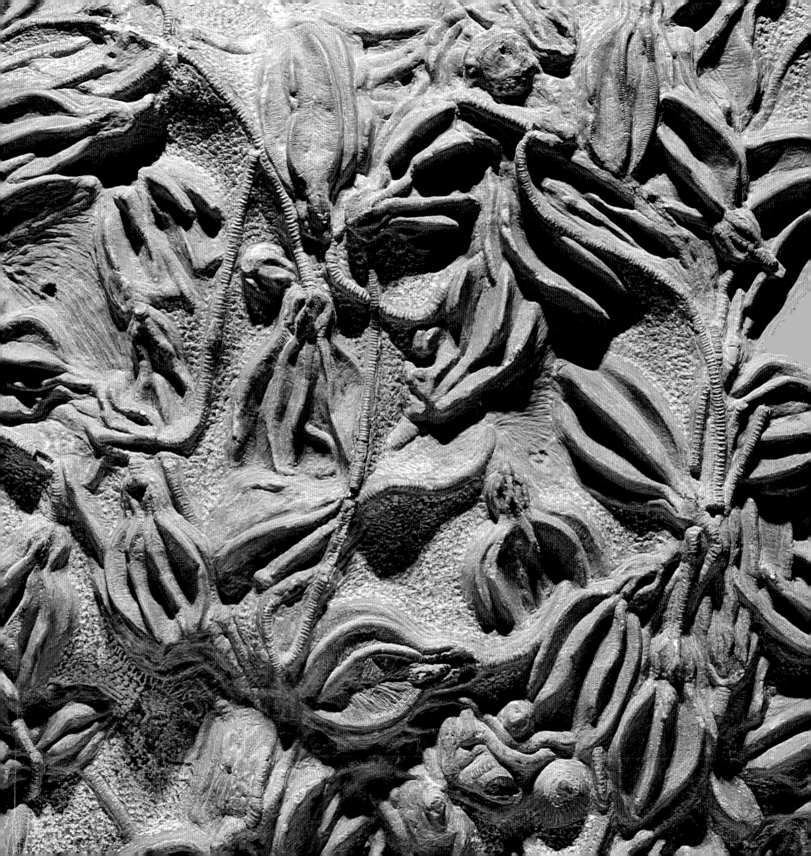

FOSSIL
F A C T

Some of the most fascinating fossils have come from the Smoky Hill Chalk, near Hays, Kansas. There you'll find fish, marine reptiles, flying reptiles, and birds.

Scientists in other fields rely on the fossil record to help them in their studies. Paleoecology is the study of plant and animal relationships with their environments. By examining the fossil record, researchers were able to tell that the growth of certain grasses in particular areas affected the evolution of grass-eating **mammals.**

Above, fish fossil

Left, a trilobite; above, Chalk Cliffs of Dover in Kent, England

Paleogeography is the study of plants and animals in relation to their locations on earth. Scientists in this field can study fossils to tell why certain plants and animals live only in certain areas of the world today. They can also learn why some kinds of animals **migrate.**

FOSSIL
FEATHERS

Fossils recently discovered in China reveal a creature with primitive feathers along its neck, back and tail; it was about the size of a turkey with a lizard-like tail.

Right, archaeopterix

The field of paleobiology relies on fossils to study the evolution of animal species. For example, these researchers study the archaeopterix *(ARK-ee-op-ter-ix)*, the world's oldest bird, in order to understand the **transition** from flightless reptiles to winged birds. They also study whale fossils to uncover the mysteries of how some mammals developed the ability to swim and live in water.

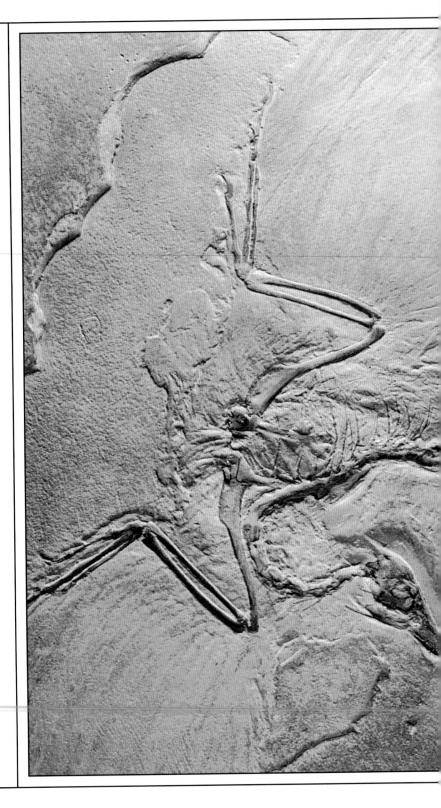

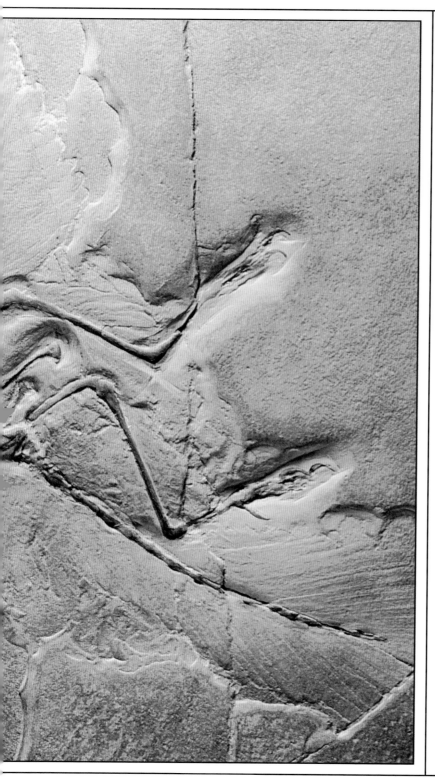

FOSSIL
F A C T

Dinosaur fossils have been discovered on every continent of the world, and they continue to be found. Many of the most famous fossils were uncovered accidentally. The very first dinosaur fossil discovered in the United States was found in 1802 by a farmer digging in his field. Across the ocean, in 1811, a 12-year-old English girl found the first ichthyosaur *(IK-thee-o-sawr).*

The hard crusts of plant spores and pollen grains form most of the body fossils common in layered rock.

Below, fish fossil in limestone

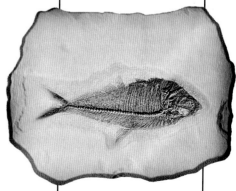

FOSSIL

FAMILY

The Mesolimulus *horseshoe crab, which lived 150 million years ago, evolved into the* Limulus *horseshoe crab, which is still alive today.*

Above, modern horse-shoe crab; right, horseshoe crab fossil

This girl, Mary Anning, went on to find two more incredible dinosaur fossils—a plesiosaur *(PLES-ee-o-sawr)* in 1821 and a pterosaur *(TER-o-sawr)* in 1828.

While digging out limestone for industrial use, workers in the Solnhofen quarry in southern Germany discovered large numbers of ancient jellyfish, horseshoe crabs, flying reptiles, and even an archaeopterix.

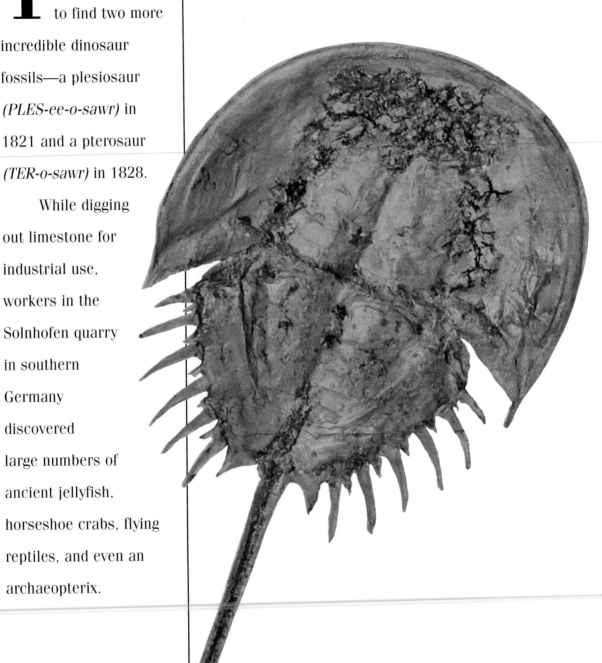

FOSSIL

FLOWER

The magnolia is the modern relative of the first flowering plant on earth, which appeared 130 million years ago.

In 1909, dinosaur remains were found in a sandstone outcropping at a site located on the Colorado-Utah border. Six years later this place became Dinosaur National Monument.

Fossil Butte National Monument, in southwestern Wyoming, is home to thousands of fossils from 65 million to 40 million years ago. Known as Fossil Basin, the site contains the remains of fish, plants, insects, and even early mammals.

Left, dinosaur head being excavated; above, petroglyphs, or cave drawings, at Dinosaur National Monument

FOSSIL

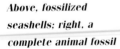

EARLY

The first animals to evolve were very simple. Fossils of early jellyfish are dated to 600 million years ago, and the first shellfish appeared 50 million years later.

Above, fossilized seashells; right, a complete animal fossil

LIVING FOSSILS

Most of the prehistoric species found in fossils are **extinct.** Some of them, however, have evolved into species alive today. **Amphibians,** such as frogs and toads, and reptiles, such as the Galapagos tortoise evolved from ancient species of animals.

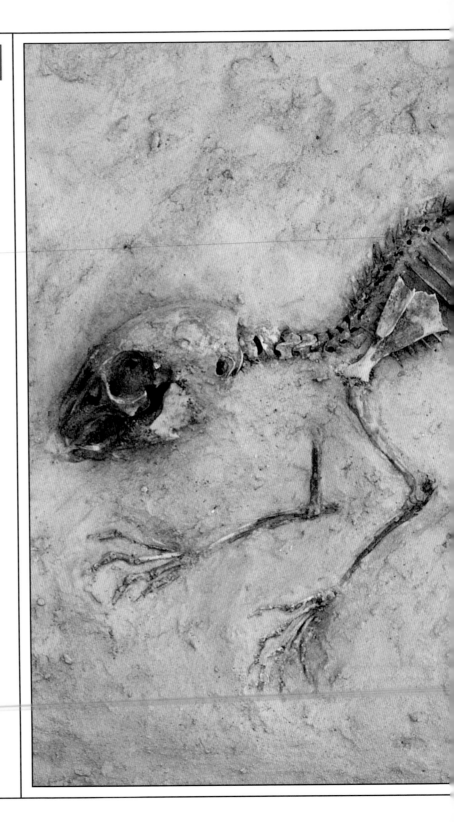

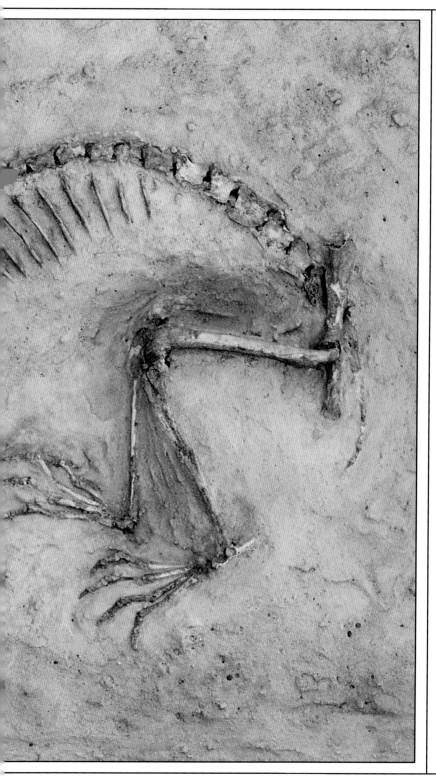

Some plants and animals have hardly changed at all from their ancient relatives. Sea lilies, starfish, and sea sponges look just the same as their prehistoric ancestors once did. They are called "living fossils." Scientists know that other "living fossils," such as the dragonfly, crocodile, cockroach, and ginkgo tree, existed in prehistoric times because they have discovered fossil remains of these things.

FOSSIL
FACT

Small sea animals first evolved to live on land 400 million years ago. Fossils tell us that these creatures evolved into modern spiders and insects.

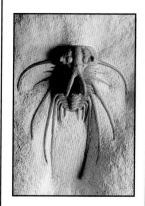

Above, a trilobite

FOSSIL
GIANT

The Megatherium, *or giant ground sloth, was bigger than a modern-day elephant. It became extinct 11,000 years ago, but its relative, the three-toed sloth of South America, still exists.*

FOSSIL
CROC

An ancient ancestor of the modern crocodile was the Macroplata, *a 15-foot-long (4.5 m) plesiosaur with a long neck and a crocodile-like snout.*

Right, coelacanth and far right, crocodiles, are both "living fossils"

An amazing "living fossil" discovery took place about 50 years ago. Scientists found fossilized remains of the 65-million-year-old coelacanth *(SEE-luh-kanth)* and assumed it was extinct. But in 1938 some fishermen netted the giant five-foot fish off the coast of Africa—very much alive! Since then, several others have been found, but their numbers are few and researchers now fear this "living fossil" may truly be near extinction.

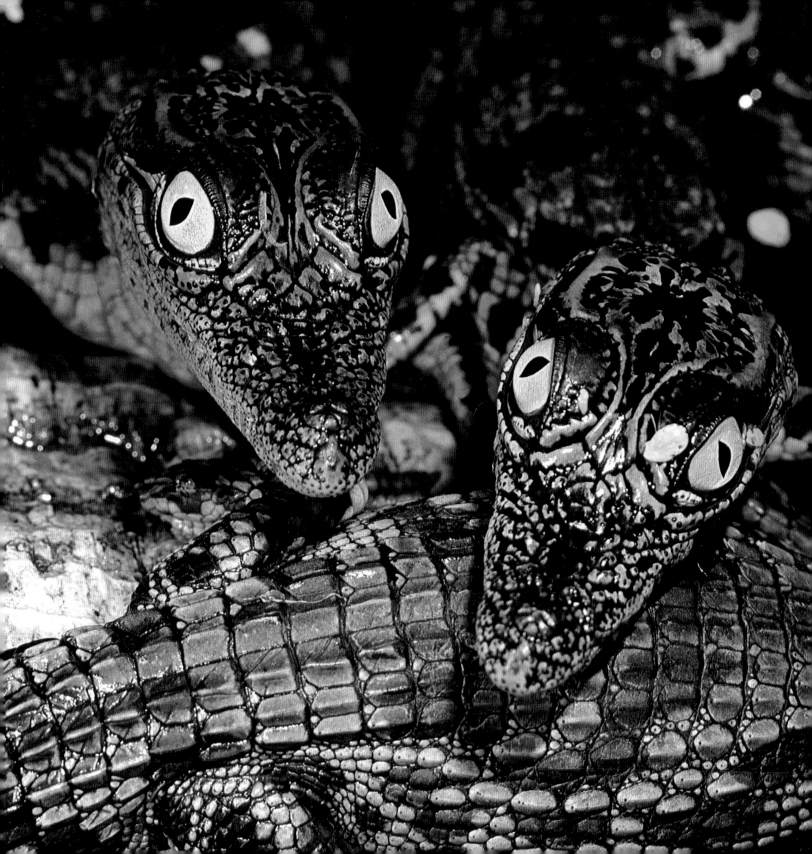

FOSSIL
F A C T

The first mammals appeared 210 million years ago. They were insect-eaters, and specimens remained no bigger than a mouse for 145 million years—until the dinosaurs died out.

Triceratops skull

FOSSIL COLLECTING

Collecting fossils can be a fun hobby if you know where to look and if you have the right equipment. Wherever fossils have been found, there are usually more waiting to be discovered.

The most important tools needed for gathering fossils are a hammer for breaking rocks; a chisel for chipping rocks; and a putty knife, spade, or trowel for loosening soil. Once you find a fossil, you will need to carefully brush away the soil with a paintbrush.

FOSSIL FACT

Fossils of the Eurypterus, or sea scorpion, indicate that this 5-inch (12.5 cm) animal became extinct 250 million years ago.

Left, fossilized fish being uncovered; above, sea scorpion fossil

FOSSIL
F A C T

The earth was formed 4.6 billion years ago, but there is no record of life on the planet until one billion years later.

FOSSIL
T H E O R Y

Some paleobiologists believe that dinosaurs were not awkward beasts, but rather warm-blooded animals that nested and cared for their young just like today's birds.

Right, cricket fossil; far right, turtle fossil

Wearing a hard hat, gloves, and goggles will protect you from sharp rocks and keep you safe. Carry a notebook to record your findings and a backpack to carry your fossils home. It is also important to mark the date and the place you made your fossil discovery.

The fossil record tells us that life on our planet is always evolving. It supports our understanding of how species develop and helps us determine the age of our planet. We can also reconstruct and study ancient ecosystems. Fossils are important keys to discovering our past and opening doors to our future.

Glossary

Amphibians are animals that usually have gilled water-breathing young and air-breathing adults and that live their whole lives in or near water.

When something is very old, it is said to be **ancient.**

Body fossils are the fossilized remains of the hard parts of an animal, like the teeth, bones, or shells.

Ecosystems are groups of plants and animals living together and helping each other to survive and grow. Ecosystems can be large, like the whole world, or very small, like a pond or forest.

When material is worn away from the earth's surface by weathering such as rain, flowing water, or wind, we call the process **erosion.**

Evolution is a process in which a plant or animal changes into a different or better form.

Plants or animals that are **extinct** have died out completely and have disappeared from the earth.

The fossilized remains of plants and animals make up the **fossil record,** which scientists use to study earth's past.

When something is **fossilized,** it has changed to stone or mineral and has become a fossil.

Imprints are made when the chemicals in a leaf or other very thin structure "print" on a rock.

Mammals are animals that feed their young with milk from the mother's body and whose skin is covered with hair or fur.

Animals that **migrate** travel from one location to another, usually because of changes in the seasons.

Minerals are substances in the earth that have color, hardness, and form crystals. Some minerals dissolve in water and then harden when they dry.

The period in the earth's history from 600 million to 225 million years ago is the **Paleozoic Era.** The name means "ancient life" in Greek.

Something becomes **petrified** when minerals dissolved in water replace the organic, or once living, matter.

Reptiles are animals that crawl on their bellies (snakes) or on small short legs (lizards) and whose bodies are covered with scales or bony plates.

Scientists studying Earth's past created a **time chart** that traces the entire history of our planet, from its birth in the universe to present day.

The remains of a plant's or animal's activity, such as a footprint, are called **trace fossils.**

When something passes from one form to another, we call the change a **transition.**

A **trilobite** is any of 4,000 species of extinct sea creatures with segmented bodies. Their fossils are found all over the world.